VHF Radio

Short Range Certificate

Syllabus & Sample Exam Questions

an **RYA** *training* publication

Updated 2002

Published by
The Royal Yachting Association
RYA House Romsey Road Eastleigh
Hampshire SO50 9YA
Tel: +44 (0)23 8062 7400
Fax: +44 (0)23 8062 9924
Email: admin@rya.org.uk
Web: www.rya.org.uk

CONTENTS

INTRODUCTION

The Short Range Certificate (SRC) is the radio operator qualification which authorises the holder to operate a VHF radiotelephone, fitted with Digital Selective Calling (DSC) on board any British vessel which is voluntarily fitted with radio equipment.

The syllabus for the SRC was designed by the Conference of European Posts and Telecommunications (CEPT), as a standard qualification for the operation of equipment using procedures and techniques of the Global Maritime Distress and Safety System (GMDSS).

If you do not hold a certificate there are two ways to obtain the SRC. It can be awarded either on satisfactory completion of an assessed course carried out at an RYA Recognised Teaching Establishment or by taking an examination.

Courses and examinations cover all aspects of marine band VHF radio communication. Shorter courses and examinations are available for candidates who hold non-GMDSS radio operator certificates and who wish to convert to a GMDSS qualification.

Restricted (VHF only) Radio Operator Certificates of Competence issued prior to 1 September 2000 remain valid qualifications for the operation of non-GMDSS VHF radiotelephones.

To be able to answer the test questions in this book you will need to read the RYA book *VHF Radio (inc GMDSS)*. See inside front cover for more details.

THE SHORT RANGE CERTIFICATE (SRC) AWARD SYSTEM

The following arrangements apply to the award of the SRC. Certificates issued prior to the introduction of the SRC will continue to be valid for use with non-GMDSS equipment.

Courses

Teaching Establishments recognised by the RYA to conduct SRC courses, may offer courses of a minimum of eight hours duration for up to 12 students, during which students will be assessed for the award of the SRC. The course length must be extended by 15 minutes for each additional student. Courses leading to the award of the SRC for students who already hold a non-GMDSS certificate, must be a minimum of three hours duration for up to 12 students, again adding 15 minutes for each additional student.

These assessed courses must be conducted by persons holding an SRC assessor qualification. There is no examination fee for students on assessed courses but a certificate issue fee will be charged. For details of the current fee, see the assessment/examination application form. Details of the RYA Training Centres can be found on the RYA website: www.rya.org.uk/training.

Examinations

Those who do not wish to attend a course may take the examination for the SRC or the conversion from non-GMDSS certificate to SRC at a RYA Training Centre. Examination fees are given on the assessment/examination application form.

The syllabus

The syllabus for the SRC is set by the CEPT and full details are given in Annex A (see page 17).

Forms of assessment

On a course, assessment is a continuous process. The all-important practical assessment is complemented by a written test covering other areas of the syllabus. A list of learning outcomes to be achieved by a practical assessment, and questions to be used in the written test are given from page 5. There are four ways to get a Short Range Certificate:

1. For those with no certificate - attend a full course run by a RYA Training Centre during which assessment will be carried out.
2. For those with a non-GMDSS certificate - attend a short course run by a RYA Training Centre during which assessment will be carried out.
3. For those with no certificate who do not wish to attend a course - apply to a RYA Training Centre for a full SRC examination.
4. For those with a non-GMDSS certificate who do not wish to attend a course - apply to a RYA Training Centre for an SRC conversion examination.

Application forms and supporting documents

Assessment/examination application forms can be obtained from the RYA, or a RYA Training Centre. All applicants MUST provide a passport size photograph of themselves when they return the application form.

Age limit

There is no age limit for the assessment or examination for the SRC, however, an authority to operate will not be issued to any person under the age of 16.

Quality monitoring

A system of periodic moderation of assessed courses and examinations is carried out. This includes telephone interviews to monitor the quality of teaching and assessment with a percentage of candidates willing to participate. Certificates issued prior to the introduction of the SRC will continue to be valid for use with non-GMDSS equipment.

SYLLABUS
SHORT RANGE CERTIFICATE (SRC)

OUTLINE SUMMARY

The examination consists of theory supplemented by practical tests and/or assessed practical training, and should include at least:

A General knowledge of VHF radiotelephone communications in the maritime mobile service

A1 The general principles and basic features of the maritime mobile service relevant to vessels not subject to a compulsory fit under the SOLAS Convention.

B Detailed working knowledge of radio equipment

B1 The VHF radio installation.

B2 Purpose and use of Digital Selective Calling (DSC) facilities.

C Operational procedures of the GMDSS and detailed practical operation of GMDSS subsystems and equipment

C1 Search and Rescue (SAR) Procedures in the Global Maritime Distress and Safety system (GMDSS).

C2 Distress, urgency and safety communication procedures in the GMDSS.

C3 Protection of distress frequencies.

C4 Maritime Safety Information (MSI).

C5 Alerting and Locating Signals.

D Operational procedures and regulations for VHF radiotelephone communications

D1 Ability to exchange communications relevant to the safety of life at sea.

D2 Regulations, obligatory procedures and practices.

D3 Practical and theoretical knowledge of radiotelephone procedures.

The full detailed syllabus is in Annex A (see page 17).

CONTENT OF ASSESSMENT
Assessment of Practical Ability

The student can perform the following functions:

A Distress Situations

1 Define a distress situation.

2 Initiate a DSC distress alert, with position and time input manually or automatically.

3 Send a Mayday call and message by voice.

4 Respond appropriately to a DSC distress alert and to a Mayday call and message, including relay of a distress message.

5 Deploy an EPIRB and SART.

B Urgency Situations

1 Define an urgency situation.

2 Initiate a DSC urgency alert.

3 Send a Pan Pan call and message by voice.

4 Respond appropriately to an urgency message.

C Safety Situations

1 Identify a situation in which a safety message is appropriate.

2 Initiate a DSC safety alert.

3 Send a safety message by voice.

4 Receive Maritime Safety Information by NAVTEX.

D Routine Communication

1 Initiate a DSC routine call.

2 Establish communication and exchange messages with other stations by voice on appropriate channels.

3 Test the radiotelephone by means of an appropriate test call.

4 Initiate a DSC self test.

5 Enter a DSC group and individual Maritime Mobile Service Identity (MMSI).

6 Maintain an appropriate listening watch on DSC and voice channels.

7 Use the international phonetic alphabet.

WRITTEN TEST QUESTIONS

The written test consists of:

Part A – Distress and Urgency Procedures.

Part B – General questions.

Written test papers will be formulated from the following bank of questions. Each paper will have four questions in Part A with a maximum of 11 marks and a pass mark of eight, and 11 questions in Part B with a maximum of 11 marks and a pass mark of eight.

Time allowed to complete the paper is 30 minutes.

Part A - Distress and urgency procedures

Question 1 (2 marks)

a) For which of the following would it be incorrect to initiate a DSC distress alert?

    1) A man has fallen overboard in heavy weather at night.

    2) A crew member has a broken arm and is in considerable pain.

    3) A motor cruiser has an engine failure in heavy weather close to a rocky lee shore.

b) Under what circumstances should a DSC distress alert be made?

c) Which of the following situations would warrant the issue of a DSC distress alert?

    1) You sight a series of red parachute flares far out to sea.

    2) A crew member has sustained a serious head injury, is unconscious and bleeding from the ears.

    3) You notice that a large navigational buoy has broken loose and is drifting in a strong tidal stream.

d) What type of DSC alert would you make in each of the following situations?

    1) You sight a number of wooden telephone poles floating in the middle of the English Channel. There are many other yachts in the vicinity.

    2) Total engine failure in a motor cruiser in rough weather, close to a lee shore.

    3) You sight distress flares, far out to sea.

e) Under what circumstances would you initiate a DSC urgency alert?

Question 2 (2 marks)

a) If you receive a DSC distress alert what action should you take?

b) You receive a DSC distress alert and it is acknowledged by the Coastguard. What action should you take?

c) You have accidentally sent a DSC distress alert. List the actions you would take and write the message you would send.

d) You receive a Mayday call and message on Channel 16. Your boat is fitted with a Class D DSC controller. What action should you take?

e) There is a yacht about one mile from you, it is trailing orange smoke and has a crew member standing on deck and repeatedly raising and lowering his outstretched arms. What radio alert, call and message would you send?

Question 3 (6 marks)

a) Your boat is on fire and the extinguishers have not put it out. You are on deck with your two crew, about to abandon to the liferaft. Your present position is 51°29'.2N 001°42'.7E. Write the distress call and message you would send after making a distress alert, your MMSI number is 232001457.

b) Your boat has developed a bad leak and is sinking. There are three other adults on board with you. Your present position is 49°48'.5N 005°46'.5W. Write the distress call and message you would send after making a distress alert, your MMSI number is 233000394.

c) You are alone on board, the engine of your motor cruiser has broken down and the craft is dragging her anchor towards a rocky lee shore in a gale. Your position is 50°17'.8N 004°14'.6W. Write the distress call and message you would send after making a distress alert, your MMSI number is 234000589.

d) Your boat has grounded in a north east gale on the northern end of Long Sand Head. Your position is 51°45'.8N 001°34'.5E. She is pounding heavily and you fear that she will shortly break up. On board with you are one man, one woman and two children. Your liferaft has been carried away and you have no means of abandoning the vessel. Write the distress call and message you would send after making a distress alert, your MMSI number is 232001455.

e) Your yacht has hit a submerged object and is sinking. Your position is 51°24'.8N 003°04'.4W. On board are a total of three adults. Write the distress call and message you would send after transmitting a distress alert, your MMSI number is 234001456.

Question 4 (1 mark)

a) What is the meaning of the procedure words SEELONCE MAYDAY?

b) What is the meaning of the procedure word PRUDONCE?

c) What procedure words would you use to prefix a message passing on a distress call to the Coastguard?

d) What procedure words would be used by the controlling station to indicate the end of distress working?

e) What is the meaning of the procedure words SEELONCE FEENEE?

Part B – General questions
Each question carries 1 mark.

Question 5

a) Which of the following channels is used to send a DSC All Ships safety alert?

   1) Channel 70.

   2) Channel 16.

   3) Channel 10.

   4) Channel 67.

b) Which of the following channels should be used to transmit an URGENCY message by voice?
   1) Channel 9.
   2) Channel 16.
   3) Channel 70.
   4) Channel 85.

c) A DSC All Ships urgency alert should be made:
   1) if you are in grave and imminent danger and require immediate assistance?
   2) when a new severe gale warning is issued?
   3) when you have missed the weather forecast and the wind is increasing?
   4) before sending a Mayday relay message by voice?

d) A Securité message is sent:
   1) by voice on Channel 16 after an All Ships DSC safety alert?
   2) by voice on Channel 70 after a DSC distress alert?
   3) by voice on Channel M?
   4) by voice on a working channel?

e) In order to send a Mayday relay using DSC should you:
   1) select Mayday relay on the DSC controller?
   2) send a DSC urgency alert?
   3) send a DSC Mayday alert?
   4) send a DSC individual call to HM Coastguard?

Question 6

a) Which of the following VHF channels is designated for bridge-to-bridge communication on matters of navigational safety within the GMDSS?
   1) Channel 15.
   2) Channel 70.
   3) Channel 6.
   4) Channel 13.

b) Channel 13 has been designated as the channel to be used for:
   1) bridge-to-bridge communication on matters concerning the safety of navigation?
   2) secondary use for digital selective calling?
   3) by ships engaged in underwater operations?
   4) for communication between ships and SAR helicopters?

c) On which VHF channel should small craft safety voice messages be passed to HM Coastguard?
   1) Channel 67.
   2) Channel 16.
   3) Channel 70.
   4) Channel 77.

d) In the UK Channel 67 is used:

    1) by the Queen's Harbourmaster when patrolling HM Dockyards?

    2) by HM Coastguard for small craft safety traffic?

    3) for sending digital alerts?

    4) for requesting a marina berth?

e) You wish to tell the HM Coastguard about a passage plan. On which voice channel should you pass the message?

    1) Channel 6.

    2) Channel 13.

    3) Channel 77.

    4) Channel 67.

Question 7

a) You wish to contact a boat but don't know its MMSI. Should you:

    1) make a DSC All Ships call?

    2) call the boat by name on Channel 16?

    3) call the boat by name on Channel 70?

    4) make a DSC individual call but without inserting the MMSI?

b) For the purposes of DSC, vessels are referred to by:

    1) their MMSI?

    2) their international call sign?

    3) their HIN?

    4) their name and, if necessary to avoid ambiguity, their base port?

c) Which of the following characteristics identify the MMSI of a group call?

    1) It commences with the three digit country MID.

    2) It commences with a single zero.

    3) It commences with two zeros.

    4) It ends in two trailing zeros.

d) Which of the following characteristics identify the MMSI of a coast station?

    1) It commences with the three digit country MID.

    2) It commences with a single zero.

    3) It commences with two zeros.

    4) It ends in two trailing zeros.

e) Which of the following identifies the MMSI of a coast station?

    1) 002320014

    2) 234678546

    3) 023376543

    4) 000234120

Question 8

a) Give the phonetic words for the following letters:

A   D   L
N   P   S

b) Give the phonetic words for the following letters:

B   E   M
O   R   T

c) Give the phonetic words for the following letters:

D   G   O
Q   R   X

d) Give the phonetic words for the following letters:

E   H   P
Y   I   W

e) Give the phonetic words for the following letters:

C   F   J
L   U   V

Question 9

a) Is the maximum permitted radiated power of a ship's marine band VHF radiotelephone:

1) 4 amps?

2) 25 watts?

3) 40 watts?

4) 1 amp?

b) Should the squelch control be used:

1) to remove interference due to on-board electrical equipment?

2) to reduce background noise to an acceptable level?

3) to protect the receiver loudspeaker from lightning strikes?

4) to reduce the receiver bandwidth and eliminate signals from adjacent channels?

c) Should the power used for transmission be:

1) the maximum power available in order to ensure good quality of communication?

2) the minimum power which will allow communication between the stations involved?

3) medium power so that transmission from sheltered harbours is possible?

4) low power in order to conserve the boat's battery?

d) If you are using a VHF radio with an aerial height of 10 metres and a power output of 25 watts, at what range would you expect to alert a coast station with an aerial height of 100 metres using Channel 70?

1) 4-5 miles?

2) 0-20 miles?

3) 30-40 miles?

4) 50-60 miles?

e) Is the purpose of the low power switch:

    1) to conserve the battery of the transmitting vessel?

    2) to avoid disturbance in the transmitting vessel by reducing the volume?

    3) to limit the range of transmission when working another station at close range?

    4) to dim the illumination of the user controls?

Question 10

a) When calling another ship not fitted with DSC should you call:

    1) by voice on Channel 70?

    2) on Channel M?

    3) on Channel 16 and expect the other vessel to suggest an intership working channel?

    4) direct on Channel 72 and hope he will be on that channel?

b) A call to a Port Operations Centre not fitted with DSC should be made on which Channel?

    1) Channel 6.

    2) Channel 16.

    3) Channel 72.

    4) the port operations channel.

c) Is the VHF voice distress channel:

    1) Channel 6?

    2) Channel 16?

    3) Channel 67?

    4) Channel 70?

d) A call to a UK marina to enquire about a visitor's berth should be made on:

    1) Channel 16?

    2) Channel 67?

    3) local port operations channel?

    4) Channel 80?

e) Channel M should be used for which of the following:

    1) digital distress alerting?

    2) race management and club safety boats?

    3) port operations?

    4) broadcasting tidal information?

Question 11

a) The NAVTEX service can be used:

    1) to request weather and navigational information from the Coastguard?

    2) to receive weather, navigational and safety information on a vessel at sea?

    3) to receive weather maps while at sea?

    4) to send weather reports to the Met Office?

b) Is NAVTEX:

  1) an international navigational vocabulary?
  2) a system for sending safety messages to the Coastguard?
  3) a system for converting DSC alerts to printed text?
  4) a system for receiving weather and navigational warnings whilst at sea?

c) Does NAVTEX offer:

  1) a system for the correction of electronic navigational charts?
  2) a system for receiving weather fax while at sea?
  3) a system for receiving gale warnings and navigational warnings while at sea?
  4) a system that plots the vessel's ground track?

d) Which electronic navigational aid can be interfaced with a DSC controller to input position:

  1) NAVTEX?
  2) GPS?
  3) Fluxgate compass and electronic log?
  4) Radar?

e) NAVTEX is:

  1) a chart plotting instrument?
  2) a system for receiving gale and navigation warnings?
  3) a radar alerting system?
  4) a port control system?

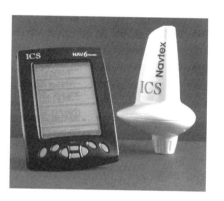

Question 12

a) With whom should you register your EPRIB?

  1) the manufacturer?
  2) the owner's shoreside contact?
  3) HM Coastguard?
  4) The Radio Communications Agency?

b) If you inadvertently activate an EPIRB, should you:

  1) throw it overboard in a weighted sack?
  2) switch it off as soon as possible?
  3) contact a Rescue Co-ordination Centre to tell them that you have activated the beacon?
  4) wrap the aerial in tinfoil to stop the signal from radiating?

c) Is a SART:

  1) a beacon which transmits distress signals through satellites?
  2) a beacon which responds to radar transmissions?
  3) a beacon which facilitates rapid transit to a man overboard?
  4) a signal to terminate search and rescue?

d) A SART should be deployed:
   1) in conjunction with a radar reflector?
   2) as close to sea level as possible?
   3) at least one metre above the sea?
   4) only in conditions of poor visibility?

e) SART stands for:
   1) Simplex Aerial for Radio Telephony?
   2) Search and Rescue Transceiver?
   3) Search Aircraft Range Transponder?
   4) Search and Rescue Transponder?

Question 13

a) Which one of the following types of call is prohibited?
   1) Call to an RNLI lifeboat.
   2) Call to a yacht club on Channel 37.
   3) Broadcast of music to other club boats.
   4) Call during the international silence periods.

b) Which one of the following types of call is permitted?
   1) Test call on Channel 80.
   2) Call without an identity.
   3) Test call on Channel 70.
   4) Hoax distress call.

c) Which one of the following types of call is permitted?
   1) Misleading distress call.
   2) Call addressed All Stations.
   3) Call containing profane or indecent language.
   4) Routine broadcast call.

d) Which one of the following calls is permitted?
   1) Call containing profane or indecent language.
   2) Call addressed to a friend at home with a handheld VHF radio.
   3) Call to a marina on Channel 80.
   4) A call on Channel 67 to another vessel about a party.

e) Is it permissible to hold a lengthy discussion on the fortunes of a football team with another vessel on an intership channel?

Question 14

a) In intership working, is communication controlled by the:
   1) calling station?
   2) station called?

MEMBERSHIP

Promoting and Protecting Boating

The RYA is the national organisation which represents the interests of everyone who goes boating for pleasure.

Personal membership is open to all boat users.

The greater the membership, the louder our voice when it comes to protecting members' interests.

Apply for membership today, and support the RYA, to help the RYA support you.

d Protecting Boating

Benefits of Membership

- Access to expert advice on all aspects of boating from legal wrangles to training matters

- Special members' discounts on a range of products and services including boat insurance, books, videos and class certificates

- Free issue of certificates of competence, increasingly asked for by everyone from overseas governments to holiday companies, insurance underwriters to boat hirers

- Access to the wide range of RYA publications, including the quarterly magazine

- Third Party insurance for windsurfing members

Look out for

- Free Internet access with RYA-Online

- A privilege price structure for purchasing a Volvo car

- The new Directions clothing and equipment catalogue

- Regular offers in RYA Magazine

Join online - plus information, advice,
member services and web shop

www.rya.org.uk

If you have previously been a member and know your membership number please enter here

When completed, please send this form to:-
Royal Yachting Association RYA House Romsey Road Eastleigh Hampshire SO50 9YA

	Tick box	Cash/Chq.	DD
Family		£44	£41
Personal		£28	£25
Under 21		£11	£11

Please indicate your main area of interest ❏ *Powerboat Racing*

❏ *Yacht Racing*   ❏ *Dinghy Cruising*   ❏ *Windsurfing*
❏ *Yacht Cruising*   ❏ *Personal Watercraft*   ❏ *Motor Boating*
❏ *Dinghy Racing*   ❏ *Inland Waterways*   ❏ *Sportsboats and RIBs*

For details of Life Membership and paying over the phone by Credit/Debit card, please call 023 8062 7400 or join online at www.rya.uk

PLEASE USE BLOCK CAPITALS

Title   Forename   Surname   Date of Birth   Male   Female

1.
2.
3.
4.

Address

Town   County   Postcode

Home Phone No.   Day Phone No.

Facsimile No.   Mobile No.

Email Address

Signature _____   Date _____

DISCOUNT IF YOU PAY BY DIRECT DEBIT - SEE ABOVE

RYA

Instructions to your Bank or Building Society to pay by Direct Debit

DIRECT Debit

Please fill in the form and send to:
Royal Yachting Association RYA House Romsey Road Eastleigh Hampshire SO50 9YA Tel: 023 8062 7400

Name and full postal address of your Bank/Building Society

To The Manager	Bank/Building Society
Address	
	Postcode

Name(s) of Account Holder(s)

Bank/Building Society account number

Branch Sort Code

Originator's Identification Number

9	5	5	2	1	3

Reference Number

Instruction to your Bank or Building Society
Please pay Royal Yachting Association Direct Debits from the account detailed in this instruction subject to the safeguards assured by The Direct Debit Guarantee. I understand that this instruction may remain with the Royal Yachting Association and, if so, details will be passed electronically to my Bank/Building Society.

Signature(s)

Date

Banks and Building Societies may not accept Direct Debit Instructions for some types of account

---

OR YOU CAN PAY BY CHEQUE

Source Code			
077	Cheque enclosed £	Made payable to the Royal Yachting Association	**Office use only:** Membership number allocated

b) Which of the following procedure words would be correct at the termination of working?

   1) Over.

   2) Over and out.

   3) Out.

   4) Logging off.

c) How would you end a transmission for which you expect a reply?

   1) Out.

   2) Over and out.

   3) Come in.

   4) Over.

d) Call signs and MMSI numbers are allocated by:

   1) The National Radio Licensing Authority?

   2) The MCA?

   3) The RYA?

   4) Harbour Master?

e) Is it permitted to pass on information gained by listening to a radio conversation between two ships:

   1) Yes?

   2) No?

Question 15

a) Under whose control may members of the crew use the radiotelephone?

   1) The skipper of the boat.

   2) The holder of a Certificate of Competence and Authority to Operate.

   3) The Owner of the ship's licence.

   4) Any responsible person aged 18 and over.

b) Under whose authority is a distress alert made?

   1) The skipper.

   2) The licenced radio operator.

   3) The Coastguard.

   4) Any concerned crew member.

c) For how long is a ship's radio licence valid?

   1) Five years.

   2) Life of the vessel.

   3) Two years.

   4) One year.

d) Who is the issuing authority for Ship Radio Licences?

    1) The RYA?

    2) The Home Office?

    3) The Radiocommunications Agency?

    4) British Telecom?

e) Can a non-DSC handheld radio be used in the tender under the authority of the parent vessel's Ship Radio Licence?

    1) Yes.

    2) No.

ANNEX A

SYLLABUS FOR THE SHORT RANGE CERTIFICATE IN DETAIL

A The general principles and basic features of the maritime mobile service relevant to vessels NOT subject to a compulsory fit under the SOLAS convention.

A1 Types of communication of the maritime mobile service.
    Distress, urgency and safety communications.
    Public correspondence.
    Port operations service.
    Ship movement service.
    Intership communication.
    On board communications.

A2 Types of station in the maritime mobile service.
    Ship stations.
    Coast stations.
    Pilot stations, port stations etc.
    Aircraft stations.
    Rescue Co-ordination Centres (RCC).

A3 Elementary knowledge of radio frequencies and channels appropriate to the VHF maritime mobile band.
    The concept of frequency.
    Propagation on VHF frequencies.
    Range for voice communications.
    Range for DSC transmissions.
    The usage of VHF frequencies in the maritime mobile service.
    The concept of radio channel: simplex, semi-duplex and duplex.
    Channel plan for VHF, including allocations for the GMDSS.
    Distress and safety channels.
    National channels for small craft safety.
    Intership communications.
    Ship movement.
    Calling channels.
    Public correspondence channels.

A4 Functionality of ship station equipment.

Sources of energy of ship stations.

Batteries: types and characteristics, charging, maintenance.

B Detailed working knowledge of radio equipment

B1 The VHF radio installation.

1.1 Radiotelephone channels.

Channel selection and controls.

Dual watch facilities and controls.

1.2 Basic controls and usage eg:

Connecting and power.

Press to transmit switch.

High/low output power switch.

Volume control.

Squelch control.

Dimmer.

1.3 Portable two-way VHF radiotelephone apparatus.

1.4 Maritime VHF antennas.

B2 Purpose and use of Digital Selective Calling (DSC) facilities.

2.1 The general principles and basic features of DSC.

DSC messages.

DSC attempt.

Call acknowledgement.

Call relay.

2.2 Types of call

Distress call.

All ships call.

Call to individual station.

Geographical area call.

Group call.

2.3 The Maritime Mobile Service Identity (MMSI) number system.

Nationality identification: Maritime Identification Digits (MID)

Ship station numbers.

Coast station numbers.

2.4 Call categorisation and priority.

Distress.

Urgency.

Safety.

Ship's business.

Routine.

2.5 Call telecommand and traffic information.

   Distress alerts.

   Other calls.

   Working channel information.

2.6 VHF DSC facilities and usage.

   Channel 70 instant alert selector.

   DSC data entry and display.

   Updating vessel position.

   Entering pre-set message.

   Entering traffic information.

   Reviving received messages.

   DSC watch keeping functions and controls.

C Operational procedures of the GMDSS and detailed practical operation of GMDSS subsystems and equipment.

C1 Search and Rescue (SAR) Procedures in the Global Maritime Distress and Safety System (GMDSS).

1.1 Sea Areas and access to GMDSS facilities.

1.2 The role of RCCs.

1.3 Organisation of search and rescue.

C2 Distress, urgency and safety communication procedures in the GMDSS.

2.1 Distress communications via VHF DSC equipment.

   DSC distress alert.

   The definition of a distress alert.

   Transmission of a distress alert.

   Transmission of a shore-to-ship distress alert relay.

   Transmission of a distress alert by a station not itself in distress.

   Receipt and acknowledgement of VHF DSC distress alert.

   Acknowledgement procedure.

   Receipt and acknowledgement by a coast station.

   Handling of distress alerts.

   Preparations for handling of distress traffic.

   Distress traffic terminology.

   On-scene communications.

   SAR operation.

2.2 Urgency and Safety communications via DSC equipment.

   The meaning of urgency and safety communications.

   Procedures for DSC urgency and safety calls.

   Urgency communications.

   Safety communications.

C3 Protection of distress frequencies.
    3.1 Avoiding harmful interference.
        Avoiding the transmission of false alerts.
        Status of Channel 70.
    3.2 Transmission during distress traffic.
    3.3 Prevention of unauthorised transmissions.
    3.4 Test protocols and procedures.
        Testing DSC equipment.
        Radiotelephone test procedures.
    3.5 Avoidance of transmissions in VHF guard bands.
    3.6 Procedures to follow when a false distress alert is transmitted.

C4 Maritime Safety Information.
    4.1 The NAVTEX system.
        Purpose and capabilities, including distress and safety functions.

C5 Alerting and Locating Signals.
    5.1 Purpose and definition.
    5.2 Emergency Position Indication Radio Beacons (EPIRBs).
        Registration and coding.
        Operation, including automatic and manual activation.
        COSPAS/SARSAT 406 MHz EPIRB.
        Inmarsat-E 1.6 GHz EPIRB.
        VHF-DSC EPIRB.
        121.5MHz homing function.
        Mounting considerations.
        Routine maintenance.
        Testing.
        Checking battery expiry date.
        Checking the float-free mechanism.
    5.3 Search and Rescue Radar Transponder (SART).
        Operation.
        Operating height.
        Effect of radar reflector.
        Range of a SART transmitter.

D Operational procedures and regulations for VHF radiotelephone communications.

D1 Ability to exchange communications relevant to the safety of life at sea.
    1.1 Distress communications.
        Distress signal.
        The correct use and meaning of the signal MAYDAY.

Distress call.

Distress message.

Acknowledgement of a distress message.

Obligation to acknowledge a distress message.

Correct form of acknowledgement.

Action to be taken following acknowledgement.

The control of distress traffic.

The correct use and meanings of the signals.

SEELONCE MAYDAY.

SEELONCE DISTRESS.

PRUDONCE.

SEELONCE FEENEE.

Transmission of a distress message by a station not itself in distress.

The correct use and meaning of the signal MAYDAY RELAY.

1.2 Urgency communications.

Safety signal.

The correct use and meaning of the signal PAN-PAN.

Urgency message.

Obtaining urgent medical advice through a coast station.

1.3 Safety communications.

Safety signal.

The correct use and meaning of the signal SECURITE.

Safety message.

Special procedures for communication with appropriate national organisations on matters affecting safety.

1.4 Reception of MSI by VHF radiotelephone.

1.5 Awareness of the existence and use of the IMO Standard Marine Navigational Vocabulary.

Knowledge of the following basic signals:

ALL AFTER; ALL BEFORE;

CORRECT; CORRECTION;

IN FIGURES; IN LETTERS;

I SAY AGAIN; I SPELL;

OUT; OVER; RADIO CHECK;

READ BACK; RECEIVED;

SAY AGAIN; STATION CALLING;

TEXT; TRAFFIC; THIS IS; WAIT;

WORD AFTER; WORD BEFORE;

WRONG.

1.6 Use of the international phonetic alphabet.

D2 Regulations. Obligatory procedures and practices.

    2.1 Awareness of international documentation and availability of national publications.

    2.2 Knowledge of the international regulations and agreements governing the maritime mobile service.

    Requirement for Ship Station Licence.

    Regulations concerning control of the operation of radio equipment by the holder of an appropriate certificate of competence.

    National regulations concerning radio record keeping.

    Preservation of the secrecy of correspondence.

    Types of call and types of message which are prohibited.

D3 Practical and theoretical knowledge of radiotelephone call procedures.

    3.1 Method of calling a Coast Station by radiotelephony.

    Ordering a manually switched link-call.

    Ending the call.

    Calls to ships from Coast Stations.

    Special facilities of calls.

    Method of calling a Coast Station DSC for general communications.

    Selecting an automatic radiotelephone call.

    3.2 Traffic charges.

    International charging system.

    Accounting Authority Identification Code (AAIC).

    3.3 Practical traffic routines.

    Correct use of call signs.

    Procedure for establishing communication on:

        intership, public correspondence, small craft safety, port operations and ship movement channels.

    Procedure for unanswered calls and garbled calls.

    Control of communications.

EXTRACT FROM MARITIME GUIDANCE NOTE MGN22 (M+F)

Proper Use of VHF Channels at Sea

1. The International Maritime Organisation (IMO) has noted with concern the widespread misuse of VHF channels at sea especially the distress, safety and calling Channels 16 (156.8 MHz) and 70 (156.525 MHz), and channels used for port operations, ship movement services and reporting systems. Although VHF at sea makes an important contribution to navigational safety, its misuse causes serious interference and, in itself, becomes a danger to safety at sea. IMO has asked Member Governments to ensure that VHF channels are used correctly.

2. All users of marine VHF on United Kingdom vessels, and all other vessels in United Kingdom territorial waters and harbours, are therefore reminded, in conformance with international and national legislation, marine VHF apparatus may only be used in accordance with the International Telecommunication Union's (ITU) Radio Regulations. These Regulations specifically prescribe that:

    (a) Channel 16 may only be used for distress, urgency and very brief safety communications and for calling to establish other communications which should then be concluded on a suitable working channel;

    (b) Channel 70 may only be used for Digital Selective Calling not oral communication;

    (c) On VHF channels allocated to port operations or ship movement services such as VTS, the only messages permitted are restricted to those relating to operational handling, the movement and the safety of ships and to the safety of persons;

    (d) All signals must be preceded by an identification, for example the vessel's name or call sign;

    (e) The service of every VHF radio telephone station shall be controlled by an operator holding a certificate issued or recognised by the station's controlling administration, normally the vessel's country of registration. Providing the station is so controlled, other persons besides the holder of the certificate may use the equipment.

3. Appendix 1 to this notice consists of notes on guidance on the use of VHF at sea and is an extract from IMO Resolution A.474(XII). Masters, Skippers and Owners are urged to ensure that VHF channels are used in accordance with this guidance.

4. For routine ship-to-ship communications, the following channels have been made available in United Kingdom waters: 6, 8, 72 and 77. Masters, Skippers and Owners are urged to ensure that all ship-to-ship communications working in these waters are confined to these channels, selecting that most appropriate in the light of local conditions at the time. All other channels are allocated to the Port Operations, Ship Movement or Public Correspondence Services and may only be used for this purpose.

5. Channel 13 is designated for use on a world-wide basis as a navigation safety communication channel, primarily for intership navigation safety communications. It may also be used for the ship movement and port services subject to the national regulations of the administrations concerned.

6. Typical VHF ranges are contained in the example at Appendix II. It must be noted however that under some circumstances these 'typical' ranges may not be achieved.

7. A Table of Transmitting Frequencies in the band 156 – 174MHz for Stations in the Maritime Mobile Service is shown at Appendix III.

Marine Safety Agency, Spring Place, 105 Commercial Road, Southampton SO15 1EG

RYA Note: Appendixes 2 and 3 are not included in this book.

APPENDIX I TO MGN22 (M+F)

Guidance on the use of VHF at sea

1) PREPARATION

Before transmitting, think about the subjects which have to be communicated and, if necessary, prepare written notes to avoid unnecessary interruptions and ensure that no valuable time is wasted on a busy channel.

2) LISTENING

Listen before commencing to transmit to make certain that the channel is not already in use. This will avoid unnecessary and irritating interference.

3) DISCIPLINE

VHF equipment should be used correctly and in accordance with the Radio Regulations. The following in particular should be avoided:

(a) calling on Channel 16 for purposes other than distress, urgency and very brief safety communications when another calling channel is available;

(b) communication on Channel 70 other than for Digital Selective Calling;

(c) communications not related to safety and navigation on port operation channels;

(d) non-essential transmissions, e.g. needless and superfluous signals and correspondence;

(e) transmitting without correct identification;

(f) occupation of one particular channel under poor conditions;

(g) use of offensive language.

4) REPETITION

Repetition of words and phrases should be avoided unless specifically requested by the receiving station.

5) POWER REDUCTION

When possible, the lowest transmitter power necessary for satisfactory communication should be used.

6) COMMUNICATIONS WITH SHORE STATIONS

Instructions given on communication matters by shore stations should be obeyed.

Communications should be carried out on the channel indicated by the shore station. When a change of channel is requested, this should be acknowledged by the ship.

On receiving instructions from a shore station to stop transmitting, no further communications should be made until otherwise notified (the shore station may be receiving distress or safety messages and any other transmissions could cause interference).

7) COMMUNICATIONS WITH OTHER SHIPS

During ship-to-ship communications the ship called should indicate the channel on which further transmissions should take place. The calling ship should acknowledge acceptance before changing channel.

The listening procedure outlined above should be followed before communications are commenced on the chosen channel.

8) DISTRESS COMMUNICATIONS

Distress calls/messages have absolute priority over all other communications. When hearing them all other transmissions should cease and a listening watch should be kept.

Any distress call/message should be recorded in the ship's log and passed to the master.

On receipt of a distress message, if in the vicinity, immediately acknowledge receipt. If not in the vicinity, allow a short interval of time to elapse before acknowledging receipt of the message in order to permit ships nearer to the distress to do so.

9) CALLING

Whenever possible, a working frequency should be used. If a working frequency is not available, Channel 16 may be used, provided it is not occupied by a distress call/message.

In case of difficulty to establish contact with a ship or shore station, allow adequate time before repeating the call. Do not occupy the channel unnecessarily and try another channel.

10) CHANGING CHANNELS

If communications on a channel are unsatisfactory, indicate change of channel and await confirmation.

11) SPELLING

If spelling becomes necessary (eg. descriptive names, call signs, words which could be misunderstood) use the spelling table contained in the International Code of Signals and the Radio Regulations.

12) ADDRESSING

The words 'I' and 'You' should be used prudently. Indicate to whom they refer.

Example:

"Seaship, this is Port Radar, Port Radar, do you have a pilot?"

"Port Radar, this is Seaship, I do have a pilot."

13) WATCH KEEPING

Ships fitted with VHF equipment should maintain a listening watch on Channel 16 and, where practicable, Channel 13 when at sea.

In certain cases Governments may require ships to keep a watch on other channels.

EXTRACT FROM MARINE GUIDANCE NOTE MGN27 (M+F)

Dangers in the Use of VHF Radio in Collision Avoidance.

1. There have been a significant number of cases when it has been found that at some stage before the collision, VHF radio was being used by one or both parties in an attempt to avoid collision. The use of VHF radio in this role is not always helpful and may even prove dangerous.

2. Uncertainties can arise over the identification of vessels and the interpretation of messages received. At night, in restricted visibility or when there are more than two vessels in the vicinity the need for positive identification of the two vessels is essential but this can rarely be guaranteed. Even where positive identification has been achieved there is still the possibility of a misunderstanding between the parties concerned due to language difficulties however fluent they are in the language being used. An imprecise, or ambiguously expressed, message could have serious consequences.

3. Valuable time can be wasted while mariners on vessels approaching each other try to make contact on VHF radio instead of complying with the requirements of the Collision Regulations. There is further danger that if contact has been established, identification has been achieved and no language or message difficulty exists, a course of action is chosen which does not comply with the Collision Regulations. This can lead to the collision it was intended to avoid.

4. In 1995 the judge in a collision case said: "It is very probable that the use of VHF radio for conversation between these ships was a contributory cause of this collision, if only because it distracted the officers on watch from paying careful attention to their radar. I must repeat, in the hope that it will achieve some publicity, what I have said on previous occasions, that any attempt to use VHF to agree the manner of passing is fraught with the danger of misunderstanding. Marine superintendents would be well advised to prohibit such use of VHF radio and to instruct their officers to comply with the Collision Regulations."

5. Although the practice of using VHF radio as a collision avoidance aid may be resorted to on occasion, especially in pilotage waters, the risks described in this Note should be clearly understood and the Collision Regulations complied with.

Maritime and Coastguard Agency
Spring Place, 105 Commercial Road, Southampton SO15 1EG
Tel: 023 8032 9100   Fax: 023 8032 9161

August 1997

ANNEX C

EXTRACT FROM MARINE INFORMATION NOTICE 63 (M+F)

Maritime Distress watch by HM Coastguard

1. Background

Under the Global Maritime Distress and Safety System (GMDSS) vessels subject to the Safety of Life at Sea (SOLAS) Convention were to have converted to GMDSS communications from 1 February 1999. In terms of VHF and MF Distress communications, this meant having the capability to alert rescue services (in the UK, HM Coastguard) electronically through VHF and MF Digital Selective Calling (DSC). Once an alert is received by the rescue services they would talk to the distressed vessel an the designated distress frequency (Channel 16 or 2182kHz). HM Coastguard is fully equipped to deal with VHF and MF DSC alerts.

2. VHF Distress Watch

The IMO Maritime Safety Committee (MSC) agrees to defer the GMDSS implementation date for VHF DSC until 1 February 2005 but, through IMO Resolutions that GMDSS vessels should continue to maintain a continuous VHF Distress watch when practicable. This has now been implemented through Merchant Shipping (Radio Installation) Regulations 1998, which came into force on 28 September 1998. To align with the IMO decision and MS Regulations, it was considered appropriate that the MCA should announce that Coastguard will cease its dedicated headset VHF Distress watch on 31 January 2005.

3. It is important to note that ceasing the dedicated VHF Distress watch does not dispense with the Coastguard capability to monitor the VHF Distress channel, since the channel is still needed to talk to a distressed vessel after the GMDSS DSC electronic alert. It is also still required to maintain communications with other ships assisting in the distress situation. Therefore, after 31 January 2005, Coastguard will keep a 'loudspeaker' watch on the VHF Distress channel.

4. MF Distress Watch

The MF Distress watch cut-off date of 1 February 1999 proceeded on schedule. However, fishing vessels, which are subject to different radio regulations than SOLAS GMDSS ships, are required to keep a MF Distress watch until 1 January 2002 (when the relevant MS regulations will change). A dedicated (desk-bound) 2182kHz Distress watch will need to be maintained by HM Coastguard until 31 March 2002. Thereafter, HM Coastguard will revert to an 'ambient' loudspeaker watch on 2182kHz. That means that there will not be an officer sat specifically in front of the radio equipment listening to the loudspeaker.

5. The long lead-in times being allowed by the MCA for the introduction of these measures, particularly with VHF, are sufficient to allow plenty of time for all types of vessel to comply with GMDSS. Moreover, the distress frequencies themselves are not being dispensed with nor is HM Coastguard's capability to monitor them.

6. Any enquiries regarding this MIN should be directed to:

Maritime and Coastguard Agency
Coastguard Operations, Spring Place, 105 Commercial Road, Southampton SO15 1EG
Telephone: 023 8032 9419   Fax: 023 8032 9488